ZAK'S ROBOT

Written by
KATE RUTTLE

Illustrated by
CHRIS EMBLETON-HALL

WAYLAND

First published in 2011
by Wayland

Text copyright © Kate Ruttle 2011

Illustration copyright © Wayland 2011

Wayland
338 Euston Road
London NW1 3BH

Wayland Australia
Level 17/207 Kent Street
Sydney, NSW 2000

Series editor: Louise John
Editor: Katie Woolley
Designer: Paul Cherrill
Consultant: Kate Ruttle

A CIP catalogue record for this book is available
from the British Library.

ISBN 9780750263924

Printed in China

Wayland is a division of Hachette Children's Books,
an Hachette UK company. www.hachette.co.uk

Fizz Wizz Phonics is a series of fun and exciting books, especially designed to be used by children who have not yet started to read.

The books support the development of language, exploring key speaking and listening skills, as well as encouraging confidence in pre-reading skills.

ZAK'S ROBOT is all about oral segmenting. Segmenting is an important skill children need in order to begin to start spelling and writing words. Segmenting happens when you see or hear a word and you **segment** (separate) the individual sounds that make up that word in order to be able to spell it. When doing segmenting activities with children, it is important to recognise that words can be broken down into individual sounds, for example sh.ee.p has three sounds, and not six.

This book encourages children to begin to hear the individual sounds in words. Throughout the book Zeek, the robot, speaks in sounds. Read aloud what Zeek says with your child, saying the sounds in the word, rather than the letter names or the full words.

When you read Zeek's words, try to read them in a creaky robot voice, and encourage your child to do the same. Children will have fun learning that words can be broken down into individual sounds to make them easier to spell and write.

For suggestions on how to use **ZAK'S ROBOT** and for further activities, look at page 24 of this book.

It was night time and Zak was tucked
up in bed. He was reading a book
about a robot world.

"See you in the morning," said Mum,
and she gave him a kiss.

Segment:
hello is **h.e.ll.o**
Zak is **Z.a.k**

When Zak woke up in the morning, he was in the robot world! A robot was standing next to him.

6

"Hello," said Zak.
"**H.e.ll.o, Z.a.k,**" said the robot.

Segment:
socks is **s.o.ck.s**
shoes is **sh.oe.s**
coat is **c.oa.t**

s.o.ck.s

Zeek, the robot, opened up the wardrobe and gave Zak some new robot clothes to wear.

c.oa.t

sh.oe.s

"Are these for me?" asked Zak.
"S.o.ck.s, sh.oe.s,
c.oa.t!" said Zeek.

e.gg.s

Zak and Zeek went downstairs
to the kitchen to eat breakfast.
Mum gave them some eggs.

"I'm hungry," said Zak.

"E.gg.s, t.oa.s.t, m.i.l.k," said Zeek.

c.ar

After breakfast, it was time for
Zak and Zeek to walk to school.
The road was very busy.

"That's a funny car!" said Zak.
"C.ar, b.u.s, b.i.ke," said Zeek.

Segment:
robot is **r.o.b.o.t**
school is **s.ch.oo.l**

r.o.b.o.t

Zak and Zeek soon arrived
at school. Zak had never
seen anything like it before!

14

s.ch.oo.l

"Is this your school?" asked Zak.

"R.o.b.o.t S.ch.oo.l!" nodded Zeek.

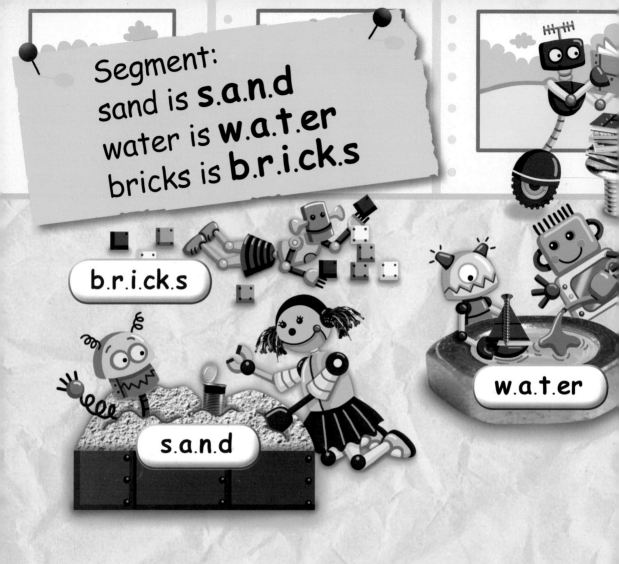

Segment:
sand is **s.a.n.d**
water is **w.a.t.er**
bricks is **b.r.i.ck.s**

b.r.i.ck.s

w.a.t.er

s.a.n.d

The teacher, Mrs Metal, showed Zak where all the toys were kept. There were lots to choose from.

"Can I play in the sand?" asked Zak.
"S.a.n.d, w.a.t.er, b.r.i.ck.s!"
said Zeek.

Segment:
pins is **p.i.n.s**
nuts is **n.u.t.s**
bolts is **b.o.l.t.s**

n.u.t.s

p.i.n.s

Then it was time for a snack.
Mrs Metal gave the children
some pins, nuts and bolts to eat.

b.o.l.t.s

"I'm not sure I like pins," said Zak.

"P.i.n.s, n.u.t.s, b.o.l.t.s," said Zeek.

19

Segment:
swing is **s.w.i.ng**
slide is **s.l.i.de**
scooter is **s.c.oo.t.er**

s.w.i.ng

After their snack, Zak and Zeek
went outside to play. Zak liked
the swing best of all.

s.l.i.de

"I like playing outside!" said Zak.
"S.w.i.ng, s.l.i.de, s.c.oo.t.er!"
laughed Zeek.

Segment:
mum is **m.u.m**
dad is **d.a.d**
home is **h.o.me**

It had been a long day. Zak was sleepy
so Zeek tucked him up in bed.
"I miss home," said Zak.

"**M.u.m, D.a.d, h.o.me,**" said Zeek.
Zak woke up back at home.
"Goodbye, Zeek," he smiled.

Further Activities

These activities can be used when reading the book one-to-one, or in the home.

P4 • Talk about Zak's bedroom. Is there anything in it which is the same as something in your room? Try to find three things which are the same and three which are different.

P6 • Read the sounds that Zeek says and try to blend them to make full words. What do you think Zak says in reply to Zeek?

P8 • Look at the page and talk about the items you can see in the picture. Can you say the words in robot language? Can you speak in a creaky, robot voice too?

P10 • Have a look at the picture. What other rooms and objects might there be in the robot house?
  • Draw pictures of other things you would see in a house like this one. Can you name the things using robot language?
  • Are there any similarities between the robot kitchen in the picture and your own kitchen at home?

P12 • Compare the robot world with things in our own world. Try to use robot language and a robot voice to say the words for the things you can see in this picture, for example c.a.r, b.u.s, b.i.ke.

P14 • Talk about the outside of the school in the picture. Why do you think Zak hadn't seen anything like it before?

P16 • Which of the robots in the picture is doing something that you would like to do?
  • Can you identify some of the activities, by saying the sounds as well as the words, for example b.r.i.ck.s is bricks; p.ai.n.t is paint.

P18 • Can you name the things in the snack trays? Try to say the sounds out loud as well as the names of the snacks.
  • Talk about why Zak is looking so unhappy.
  • Why do you think Zeek is looking happy?

P20 • Which of these playground toys would you like to play on?
  • In robot language, as well as words, name the objects in the picture, for example s.w.i.ng is swing; s.l.i.de is slide.

P22 • Talk about the ending of the story. What do you think happened to Zak and to Zeek?

These activities can be used when using the book with more than one child, or in an educational setting.

P4 • Look carefully at the cover of the book Zak is reading. How might you know that this book is about robots?
  • Think about how robots move – can you demonstrate how they might move?
  • What might a robot sound like? As a group, can you all talk like robots?

P6 • Have a look at the picture on this page. Then, as an adult re[ads] the text, try repeating what Zeek says. Can you put the sou[nds] together to make the words?
  • Look at the objects in the picture. Can you say 't.e.dd.y', 'c.ar', 'l.a.m.p', 'r.o.ck.e.t' and 'c.l.o.ck' in robot language?

P8 • Make some 'robot clothes' using cardboard boxes and rolled up newspaper. How comfortable are they? How are they like the clothes you usually wear?

P10 • Begin to make a robot world in your drama corner. Use me[tal] paper and cloth to create it. As a group, work together to d[raw] and cut out models, patterns and pictures of things you mig[ht] need in your robot house.

P12 • Use the Internet to find a picture of a street scene like this in our world.
  • Can you find similarities and differences between the two scenes.

P14 • What might you find inside a robot school? Can you suggest [some] objects and segment the words, for example teacher is t.ea[.ch.er]; toys is t.oy.s.

P16 • How does the classroom in this picture compare with your s[etting]?
  • Can you point to things in your setting that are also in this picture? Have a go at saying the sounds as well as the word[s], for example sand is s.a.n.d; water is w.a.t.er; book is b.oo.k.

P18 • Play a memory game: 'When it was snack time I had [an app]le]. The next child can continue, 'When it was snack time I had [an apple and a drink].'

P20 • Use robot language to talk about and identify all of the toys in the playground.
  • Cut out playground pictures from catalogues. Glue the pictu[res] onto some paper as you say the sounds to make up the wo[rds].

P22 • Zak has woken up back at home. Can you help him remembe[r] all the things he saw in the robot world? Try to speak in rob[ot] language as well as saying the full words.